Little Animals
Hidden Pictures

Becky Radtke

Dover Publications, Inc.
Mineola, New York

Copyright

Bibliographical Note

Little Animals Hidden Pictures is a new work, first published
by Dover Publications, Inc., in 2006.

International Standard Book Number
ISBN-13: 978-0-486-44899-2
ISBN-10: 0-486-44899-1

Manufactured in the United States by Courier Corporation
44899105   2014
www.doverpublications.com

Note

Are you ready to look for lots and lots of little animals in this fun-filled book? Each puzzle page has a picture with three or four animals hidden in it. The sentences under the picture tell you which animals are hidden—it's your job to spot each and every one! Use a pencil to shade in each animal as you find it. Some of the pictures are a bit silly—you wouldn't expect to find a giraffe in a fish tank, or a whale near a gorilla!

After you have finished each puzzle, you can check your answers in the Solutions section, which begins on page 53. Don't look until you have tried your hardest. To have even more fun, you can color all of the pictures with crayons or colored pencils. Are you ready? Let's find those hidden animals!

Mother Duck quacks "Help!" Her four ducklings have wandered off. Can you help her find them?

As this cow munches the tasty grass, she doesn't notice the three sheep hiding nearby. Try to find all three.

"Oink! Oink!" says the friendly pig. Look carefully and find the chipmunk, the lizard, and the cat in the barn.

The bunny has some friends nearby. Find the bird, the guinea pig, the fish, and the butterfly.

"Who-o-o's there?" the owl wonders. Pick out the goose, the ladybug, and the angelfish in the picture.

Four flies are buzzing around this frog. Try to find all four of them.

The bees have filled the tree with honey. The three bears would like to find the honey. Find all three bears.

The moose doesn't know that there are three squirrels close by. Can you find them?

Brrr! Polar bears love the cold! Find the three penguins that enjoy this weather, too.

Four snails are hidden at the seashore. Help the curious dog find the snails.

14

The fish in the picture really catch your eye! But look carefully and you will also find four starfish.

This tiger hears three noisy birds, but it can't see them. Take a close look and find all three.

The robins need four wiggly worms for their meal. Can you spot all four worms?

This rhino is moving too fast to see the four birds. Look all around the rhino to spot them.

The baby seal is ready for lunch. Help it find four fresh hidden fish.

A group of turtles is swimming quietly around the sleeping hippo. Can you spot all three turtles?

One of the elephants is dreaming about three animals.
Find the seal, the snake, and the jellyfish.

A bunny, a puppy, and a bat are all hiding near this roaring lion. Find all three hidden animals.

Can you find an ostrich, an octopus, and a shark surrounding the zebra in this picture?

Three animals are hidden near this leaping leopard.
Look for and find a hamster, a salamander, and a dolphin.

Is this giraffe alone in the treetops? No! Try to find four more animals—a toad, an iguana, a swan, and a fox.

These playful monkeys do not notice three animals right near them. Find the hen, the snake, and the hog.

While this mouse enjoys a treat, three animals hide in the room. Can you find the ant, the beetle, and the centipede?

The kangaroo mother and baby don't seem to see the bird, the elephant, and the iguana. Look carefully and find all three animals.

The donkey will take you for a ride! As you go along, look for the fox, the moose, and the dragonfly.

The sea turtle is a fine diver. Look carefully and spot the
four jellyfish swimming near by.

Three animals are listening as the baby penguin talks to its father. Find the dog, the alligator, and the owl.

The cougar doesn't know it, but three pigs are hidden close by. Can you spot all three pigs?

Three octopuses would like to play with the dolphin.
Find all three octopuses in this underwater scene.

The beaver is building a home in the stream. Find the
three lizards that like it there, too.

The thirsty camel has found some water! Three other animals would like a drink. Spot the pelican, the goat, and the wolf.

While this hummingbird looks for food, four beetles hide in the leaves. Look carefully and find all four.

The swimming swans are surrounded by a skunk, a lion, and a fish. Try to find all three animals.

These walruses are trying to find a dolphin, a sea turtle, and a fish. Can you spot them first?

The rooster is waking up the farm animals. Find the three kittens that already are awake.

You can almost hear this wolf as it howls! Three bats hear the wolf, too. Find all three bats.

Can you find the three animals that are sharing the fish tank with the goldfish? Look for a beetle, a lizard, and a giraffe.

The pelican thinks it's alone, but there are three animals
near it. Find the starfish, the snail, and the porcupine.

Three butterflies are fluttering around the sheep in this picture. Look carefully and find all three butterflies.

If this proud peacock looked around, it would see a snail, an opossum, and a raccoon. Can you spot all three?

Three bunnies are watching this squirrel gather acorns.
Try to find all three bunnies.

The baby goat knows that three animals are near by. Can you spot the seal, the goldfish, and the turtle?

Four friendly tree frogs are playing hide-and-seek with the parrot. Find all four frogs in this busy scene.

The gorilla is puzzled. Help it find these four hidden animals—a lizard, a rat, a porcupine, and a whale.

The alligator is swimming to the riverbank. Three snakes are slithering near the alligator. Find all three snakes.

The bird can't see the three animals that are hiding near by. Can you spot the hummingbird, the deer, and the opossum?

Ponies love to run! This pony is moving so quickly, it doesn't see the duck, the frog, and the rabbit. Can you find them?

Four mice are scurrying around as the cat naps. Try to find all four mice before the cat wakes up!

Solutions

page 5

page 6

page 7

page 8

page 9

page 10

page 11

page 12

page 13

page 14

page 15

page 16

page 17

page 18

page 19

page 20

page 21

page 22

page 23

page 24

page 25

page 26

page 27

page 28

page 29

page 30

page 31

page 32

page 33

page 34

page 35

page 36

page 37

page 38

page 39

page 40

page 41

page 42

page 43

page 44

page 45

page 46

page 47

page 48

page 49

page 50

page 51

page 52